Today the weather is...

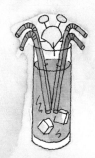

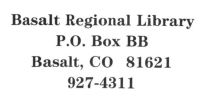

For Kate, Carly, Rowen,
Rachel, Gareth, David,
Ewan, Joseph, Eve
and . . . Sam

It's Raining, It's Pouring

A BOOK FOR RAINY DAYS

Compiled and illustrated by

Sarah Pooley

Greenwillow Books
NEW YORK

Acknowledgments

Thanks are due to the following for permission to reprint copyright material:

"I Am the Rain" from *Come on into My Tropical Garden* by Grace Nichols (A & C Black Ltd). Copyright © 1988 by Grace Nichols. Reprinted by permission of Curtis Brown Ltd. on behalf of the author.

"The Princess and the Pea" from *The Faber Book of Favourite Fairy Tales*, edited by Sara and Stephen Corrin (Faber and Faber Ltd). Copyright © 1988 by Sara and Stephen Corrin. Reprinted by permission of Faber and Faber Ltd.

"Happiness" from *When We Were Very Young* by A. A. Milne (Methuen Children's Books and Dutton Children's Books). Copyright under the Berne Convention. Copyright 1924 by E.P. Dutton, renewed 1952 by A. A. Milne. Reprinted by permission of Curtis Brown Ltd, London, and Dutton Children's Books, a division of Penguin Books U. S. A., Inc.

"Singin' in the Rain" by H. N. Brown & A. Freed. Copyright © 1929 by H. N. Brown & A. Freed. Renewed 1957 Metro-Goldwyn-Mayer, Inc. Rights assigned to Robbins Music Corp. Assigned to EMI Catalogue Partnership. All rights controlled and administered by EMI Robbins Catalog, Inc., U. S. A., EMI United Partnership Ltd, London WC2H 0EA/ International Music Publications. International copyright secured. Made in U. S. A. All rights reserved. Reprinted by permission.

"Over the Rainbow" by H. Arlen & E. Y. Harburg. Copyright © 1938, 1939 by H. Arlen & E. Y. Harburg. Renewed 1966, 1967 Metro-Goldwyn-Mayer, Inc. Assigned to Leo Feist, Inc. All rights of Leo Feist, Inc. assigned to EMI Catalogue Partnership. All rights controlled and administered by EMI Feist Catalog, Inc., U. S. A., EMI United Partnership Ltd, London WC2H 0EA/International Music Publications. International copyright secured. Made in U. S. A. All rights reserved. Reprinted by permission.

"Jonah and the Whale," "Elena and the Black Geese" and "Brer Anansi and the Rainbow's End" retold by Alison Green. Copyright © 1993 by Methuen Children's Books. Reprinted by permission of Methuen Children's Books, a division of Reed International Books.

"Weather" from *Jamboree: Rhymes for All Times* by Eve Merriam. Copyright © 1962, 1964, 1966, 1973, 1984 by Eve Merriam. Reprinted by permission of Marian Reiner for the author.

All text for activities and recipes copyright © 1993 by Sarah Pooley. Reprinted by permission of Methuen Children's Books, a division of Reed International Books.

Every effort has been made to trace all the copyright holders, and the Publishers apologize if any inadvertent omission has been made.

Library of Congress Cataloging-in-Publication Data
Pooley, Sarah.
It's raining, it's pouring : a book for rainy days/
compiled and illustrated by Sarah Pooley.
p. cm.
Summary: A collection of stories, poems, and activities
appropriate for rainy days.   ISBN 0-688-11803-8
1. Children's literature.   [1. Literature—Collections.]
I. Title   PZ5.P7646It   1993
808.8'99282—dc2o   92-16859   CIP   AC

Contents

Please remember...

When you are doing any of the activities or recipes from this book:

* Before you start, make sure you have everything you will need.
* If you are cooking, wash your hands first and put an apron on. It's a good idea to wear an apron when you are painting, too.
* Always ask an adult to help you if you are using sharp knives or scissors, or if you need to use the stove.
* Always put everything away afterward and do any washing up!

It's Raining, It's Pouring

It's raining, it's pouring.
The old man is snoring.
He went to bed
And bumped his head
And couldn't get up in the morning.

The Gingerbread Man

Once upon a time there was a little old woman and a little old man, and they lived all alone. They were very happy together, but they wanted a child and since they had none, they decided to make one out of gingerbread. So one day the little old woman and the little old man made themselves a little gingerbread man, and they put him in the oven to bake.

When the gingerbread man was done, the little old woman opened the oven door and pulled out the pan. Out jumped the little gingerbread man—and away he ran. The little old woman and the little old man ran after him as fast as they could, but he just laughed and said, "Run, run, as fast as you can. You can't catch me! I'm the Gingerbread Man!"

And they couldn't catch him.

The gingerbread man ran on and on until he came to a cow.

"Stop, little gingerbread man," said the cow. "I want to eat you."

But the gingerbread man said, "I have run away from a little old woman and a little old man, and I can run away from you, too. I can, I can!"

And the cow began to chase the gingerbread man, but the gingerbread man ran faster, and said, "Run, run, as fast as you can. You can't catch me! I'm the Gingerbread Man!"

And the cow couldn't catch him.

The gingerbread man ran on until he came to a horse.

"Please stop, little gingerbread man," said the horse. "I want to eat you."

But the gingerbread man said, "I have run away from a little old woman, a little old man, and a cow, and I can run away from you, too. I can, I can!"

And the horse began to chase the gingerbread man, but the gingerbread man ran faster and called to the horse, "Run, run, as fast as you can. You can't catch me! I'm the Gingerbread Man!"

And the horse couldn't catch him.

By and by the gingerbread man came to a field full of farmers.

"Stop," said the farmers. "Don't run so fast. We want to eat you."

But the gingerbread man said, "I have run away from a little old woman, a little old man, a cow, and a horse, and I can run away from you, too. I can, I can!"

And the farmers began to chase him, but the gingerbread man ran faster than ever and said, "Run, run, as fast as you can. You can't catch me! I'm the Gingerbread Man!"

And the farmers couldn't catch him.

The gingerbread man ran faster and faster. He ran past a school full of children.

"Stop, little gingerbread man," said the children. "We want to eat you."

But the gingerbread man said, "I have run away from a little old woman, a little old man, a cow, a horse, and a field full of farmers, and I can run away from you, too. I can, I can!"

And the children began to chase him, but the gingerbread man ran faster as he said, "Run, run, as fast as you can. You can't catch me! I'm the Gingerbread Man!"

And the children couldn't catch him.

By this time the gingerbread man was so proud of himself he didn't think anyone could catch him. Pretty soon he saw a fox. The fox looked at him and began to run after him. But the gingerbread man said, "You can't catch me! I have run away from a little old woman, a little old man, a cow, a horse, a field full of farmers, a school full of children, and I can run away from you, too. I can, I can! Run, run, as fast as you can. You can't catch me! I'm the Gingerbread Man!"

"Oh," said the fox, "I do not want to catch you. I only want to help you run away."

Just then the gingerbread man came to a river. He could not swim across, and he had to keep running.

"Jump on my tail," said the fox. "I will take you across."

So the gingerbread man jumped on the fox's tail, and the fox began to swim across the river. When he had gone a little way, he said to the gingerbread man, "You are too heavy on my tail. Jump on my back."

And the gingerbread man did.

The fox swam a little farther, and then he said, "I am afraid you will get wet on my back. Jump on my shoulder."

And the gingerbread man did.

In the middle of the river, the fox said, "Oh, dear, my shoulder is sinking. Jump on my nose, and I can hold you out of the water."

So the little gingerbread man jumped on the fox's nose, and the fox threw back his head and snapped his sharp teeth.

"Oh, dear," said the gingerbread man, "I am a quarter gone!"

Next minute he said, "Now I am half gone!"

And next minute he said, "Oh, my goodness gracious! I am three quarters gone!"

And then the gingerbread man never said anything more at all.

Little People Cookies

Makes about 12 of us!

You will need:
1 stick soft margarine
½ cup + 1 tablespoon
    light brown sugar
1 egg, beaten
1 ½ cups all-purpose flour
½ teaspoon cinnamon
½ teaspoon baking powder
currants (at least 60)

Bowl, wooden and metal spoons, sifter, plastic wrap, baking tray, knife, wire rack

1. Ask an adult to turn the oven on to 350°F.
2. Beat the margarine and sugar together in the bowl with the wooden spoon until it is light and fluffy. This takes about five minutes.
3. Beat in the egg a little at a time.
4. Sift the flour, cinnamon and baking powder together and mix into the margarine, sugar and egg mixture using a metal spoon.
5. Use your hands to form it into a firm dough and knead it lightly on a floured surface.
6. If the dough is too soft, wrap it in plastic wrap and chill it in the fridge for 20 minutes.

7. Shape the dough using your hands as follows . . .

Roll a large ball for the body, place it on the baking tray and flatten it slightly.

Roll a smaller ball for the head, attach it to the body and flatten it slightly.

Roll out small sausages of dough for the arms and legs and attach them to the body to make a person.

Press two currants onto the face for eyes and more currants on the body for buttons. With the tip of a knife make a line for the mouth.

8. Repeat until all the dough is used up, placing the people on the baking tray a little apart.

9. Bake in the oven for 15-20 minutes until they are golden.

10. Remove them from the oven and allow to cool slightly before transferring them to a wire rack. (Ask an adult to help you.)

11. Eat them up before they run away!

I Am the Rain

Grace Nichols

I am the rain
I like to play games
like sometimes
       I pretend
I'm going
       to fall
Man that's the time
I don't come at all

Like sometimes
I get these laughing stitches
up my sides
       rushing people in
and out
       with the clothesline

I just love drip
       dropping
down collars
       and spines
Maybe it's a shame
but it's the only way
I get some fame

The Three Bears

Once upon a time there were three bears who lived together in a house of their own in a wood. One of them was a little wee bear, and one was a middle-sized bear, and the third was a great big bear. They each had a bowl for their porridge—a little bowl for the little wee bear, and a middle-sized bowl for the middle-sized bear, and a great big bowl for the great big bear. And they each had a chair to sit on—a little chair for the little wee bear, and a middle-sized chair for the middle-sized bear, and a great big chair for the great big bear. And they each had a bed to sleep in—a little bed for the little wee bear, and a middle-sized bed for the middle-sized bear, and a great big bed for the great big bear.

One day, after they had made the porridge for their breakfast and poured it into their bowls, they walked out in the woods while the porridge was cooling. A little girl named Goldilocks passed by the house and looked in at the window. And then she looked in at the keyhole, and when she saw that there was no one home, she lifted the latch on the door.

The door was not locked because the bears were good bears who never did anyone any harm and never thought that anyone would harm them. So Goldilocks opened the door and walked in. She was glad to see the porridge on the table, as she was hungry from walking in the woods, and so she set about helping herself.

First she tasted the porridge of the great big bear, but that was too hot for her. Next she tasted the porridge of the middle-sized bear, but that was too cold for her. And then she tasted the porridge of the little wee bear, and that was neither too hot nor too cold but just right, and she liked it so much that she ate it all up.

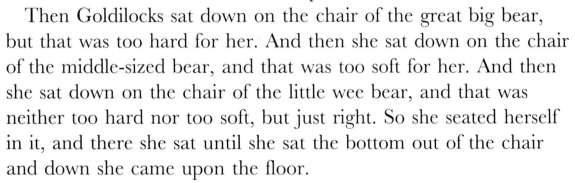

Then Goldilocks sat down on the chair of the great big bear, but that was too hard for her. And then she sat down on the chair of the middle-sized bear, and that was too soft for her. And then she sat down on the chair of the little wee bear, and that was neither too hard nor too soft, but just right. So she seated herself in it, and there she sat until she sat the bottom out of the chair and down she came upon the floor.

Then Goldilocks went upstairs to the bedroom where the three bears slept. And first she lay down upon the bed of the great big bear, but that was too high for her. And next she lay down upon the bed of the middle-sized bear, but that was too low for her. But when she lay down upon the bed of the little wee bear, it was neither too high nor too low, but just right. So she covered herself up comfortably and fell fast asleep.

When the three bears thought their porridge would be cool enough for them to eat, they came home for breakfast. Now Goldilocks had left the spoon of the great big bear standing in the porridge.

"Somebody has been eating my porridge!" said the great big bear in a great, rough gruff voice.

Then the middle-sized bear looked at its porridge and saw the spoon was standing in it, too.

"Somebody has been eating my porridge!" said the middle-sized bear in a middle-sized voice.

Then the little wee bear looked at its bowl, and there was a spoon standing in the bowl, but the porridge was all gone.

"Somebody has been eating my porridge and has eaten it all up!" said the little wee bear in a little wee voice.

Upon this, the three bears, seeing that someone had come into their house and eaten up all the little wee bear's breakfast, began to look around them.

Now Goldilocks had not put the cushion straight when she rose from the chair of the great big bear.

"Somebody has been sitting in my chair!" said the great big bear in a great, rough gruff voice.

And Goldilocks had squashed down the soft cushion of the middle-sized bear.

"Somebody has been sitting in my chair!" said the middle-sized bear in a middle-sized voice.

"Somebody has been sitting in my chair, and has sat the bottom through!" said the little wee bear in a little wee voice.

Then the three bears thought that they had better look farther in case it was a burglar, so they went upstairs into their bedroom.

Now Goldilocks had pulled the pillow of the great big bear out of its place.

"Somebody has been lying in my bed!" said the great big bear in a great, rough gruff voice.

And Goldilocks had pulled the cover of the middle-sized bear out of its place.

"Somebody has been lying in my bed!" said the middle-sized bear in a middle-sized voice.

But when the little wee bear came to look at its bed, there was the pillow in its place. But upon the pillow? There was Goldilocks' head, which was not in its place, for she had no business there.

"Somebody has been lying in my bed, and here she is still!" said the little wee bear in a little wee voice.

Now Goldilocks had heard in her sleep the great, rough gruff voice of the great big bear, but she was so fast asleep that it was no more to her than the rumbling of distant thunder. And she had heard the middle-sized voice of the middle-sized bear, but it was only as if she had heard someone speaking in a dream. But when she heard the little wee voice of the little wee bear, it was so sharp and so shrill that it woke her up at once.

Up she sat, and when she saw the three bears on one side of the bed, she tumbled out at the other and ran to the window. Now the window was open, for the bears were good, tidy bears who always opened their bedroom window in the morning to let in fresh air and sunshine. So Goldilocks jumped out through the window and ran away, and the three bears never saw anything more of her.

Teddy Bear Masks

pencil
drawing paper
crayons, paints or felt pens
scissors
string or elastic

1. Lay your paper over the teddy bear outline on the opposite page.
2. With your pencil trace round the outline.
3. Take your scissors and carefully cut around the traced-out shape.
4. Cut out the eye holes as well (you may need some help with this).
5. Color or paint your teddy bear mask.
6. Next, poke a hole in each side of the mask with your pencil.
7. Thread the string or elastic through the holes. Try the mask on and get someone to help tie a knot at the back.

Place your paper over this mask and
trace around the thick black outline

Tie elastic
through this hole

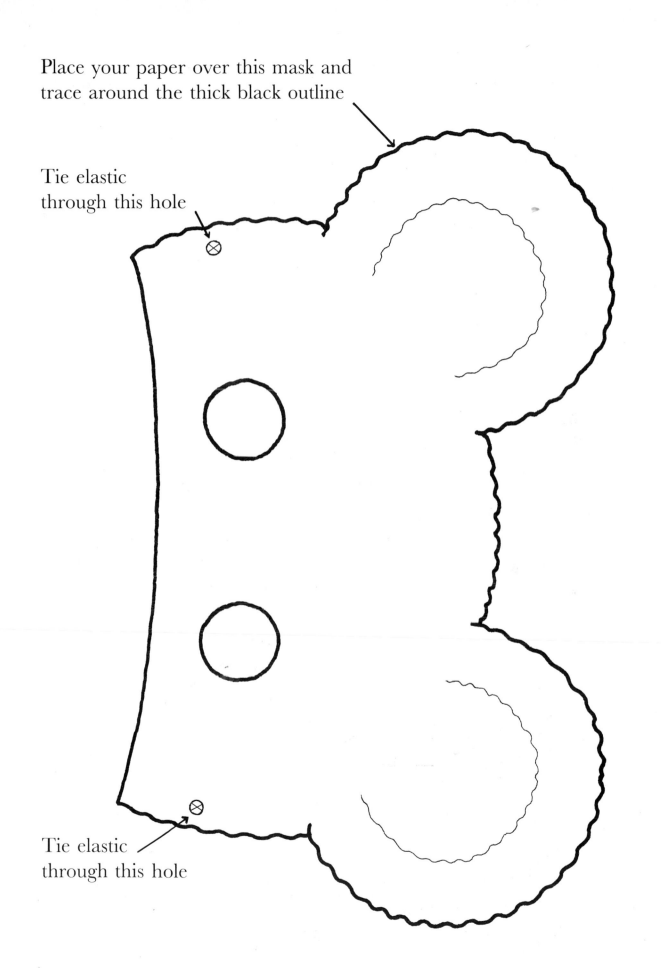

Tie elastic
through this hole

23

Toasted Cheese Bears

Today's the day the teddy bears have their picnic...if it's wet and cold outside, why not have your picnic indoors?

You will need:
4 slices of medium thick bread
butter or margarine
grated cheese (a saucerful)
six currants or raisins

This makes two bears.

Bread board, knife, mug or large cutter,
egg cup or small cutter, baking tray, plate

1. Ask an adult to turn on the broiler for you.
2. Place the slices of bread under the broiler and toast on one side until golden brown.
3. Take them out from the broiler and place on the bread board. (Ask an adult to help you.)
4. Use the mug and the egg cup (or pastry cutters) to cut two large and six small circles of toast.

5. Place the two large circles on a baking tray, toasted side down. Butter the untoasted side.

6. Put three small circles (toasted side down) on each large circle to make the bears' ears and muzzles.

7. Sprinkle the bears' faces all over with grated cheese and put the baking tray under the broiler.

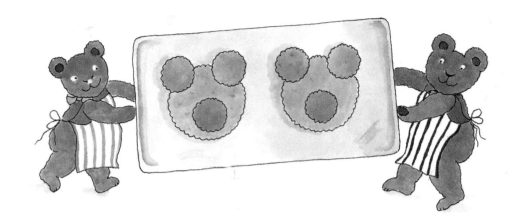

8. When the cheese is golden and melted, ask an adult to remove the bears and put them on a plate.

9. Stick two currant (or raisin) eyes and a currant nose on each bear.

10. Eat your bears while they are still warm!

Make a Weather Calendar

You will need:
scissors
paper
crayons

1. On a strip of paper draw square pictures of the weather: rain, snow, wind, sun, clouds.
2. On another piece of paper, draw a square the same size as each of your weather pictures.
3. Cut along the top and bottom edges of the square you have drawn. (You may need some help with this.)
4. Print: "Today the weather is..." above the square.
5. Slide the strip of weather pictures through the slits.

Now you can slide the strip of paper up and down to show what the weather is like each day.

Use adhesive putty to fix your picture strip onto the calendar for the day.

Today the weather is...

There are lots of sayings about the weather. You could write some of them on your weather calendar.

When the dew is on the grass,
Rain will never come to pass.

A sunshiny shower
Won't last half an hour.

The south wind brings wet weather,
The north wind wet and cold together,
The west wind always brings us rain,
The east wind blows it back again.

27

The Rainy Day Blues Band

Here's your chance to liven up a gray, drizzly day with some music . . . get your friends round to have a party!

Here are some simple instruments you can make.

Kazoo

1. Wrap a piece of thin tissue paper over a comb.
2. Now place the comb lightly against your mouth. (Make sure the tissue paper is held tightly across the comb.)
3. Hum loudly!

Glass Bottles

1. Collect lots of glass bottles all the same size and shape. (Ask an adult to help wash them.)
2. Fill each bottle with a different amount of water.
3. Lots of water in the bottle will make a high note.
4. A small amount of water in the bottle will make a low note.
5. Play the bottles by tapping gently with a pencil or a spoon — ting, ting, ting!

Shakers

1. Take two large, clean yogurt containers.
2. Half-fill each container with dried pasta or beans.
3. Put the lids on and tape them down.
4. Shake them all about!

Spoons

1. Take two spoons.
2. Hold them in one hand with the two bowls facing each other.
3. Place your index finger between the handles.
4. Knock them against your body in time with the music—clickety-clack!

Drum

1. To make a very simple drum, turn a bucket upside down.
2. Bang the bottom of the bucket with wooden spoons—Brummmm . . . tum! tum!

The Rainy Day Blues Song Book

Here are some songs to sing as you play your instruments!

I Hear Thunder

I hear thunder, I hear thunder.
Hark, don't you? Hark, don't you?
Pitter-patter raindrops,
Pitter-patter raindrops.
I'm wet through. SO ARE YOU!

Singin' in the Rain

I'm singin' in the rain, just singin' in the rain,
What a glorious feeling, I'm happy again!
I'm laughing at clouds, so dark, up above,
The sun's in my heart and I'm ready for love.
Let the stormy clouds chase ev'ry-one from the place,
Come on with the rain, I've a smile on my face.
I'll walk down the lane with a happy refrain,
And singin', just singin' in the rain.

Over the Rainbow

Somewhere over the rainbow,
Way up high,
There's a land that I've heard of
Once in a lullaby.

Somewhere over the rainbow,
Blue birds fly.
Birds fly over the rainbow,
Why then, oh why, can't I!

The Princess and the Pea

from Hans Christian Andersen, retold by Sara and Stephen Corrin

There was once a prince who wanted to marry a princess, a *truly real* princess. So off he went travelling all over the world looking for one, but there was always something that wasn't *quite* right. For although there were lots of princesses, the prince could never be absolutely certain whether they were *real* princesses or not; there was always something that didn't quite click. So back he came from his travels, very sad indeed, for he had so wanted to find a *real* princess.

One night there was a terrible storm — thunder and lightning and pouring rain — it was quite frightening. And in the middle of it all there was a violent knocking at the town gate and the old king himself went to open it. And there outside stood a princess. But goodness me! What a sight she was, what with all that wind and rain! Water ran down her hair and clothes, trickling in through the toes of her shoes and out again at the heels. But she insisted she was a *real* princess!

"We can soon find out about that!" thought the old queen, though she didn't actually say anything to the wet lady outside. She went up to the spare bedroom, removed all the bedclothes from the bed and put one pea on the bedstead. Then she got twenty mattresses, put them on top of the pea and then put a further twenty eiderdowns on top of the mattresses.

And in this bed the princess was to pass the night!

Next morning they asked her how she had slept.

"Oh, shockingly!" replied the princess. "I hardly slept a wink the whole night. I can't imagine what there was in the bed but it must have been something very hard because I'm black and blue all over. It was dreadful!"

Now they could see that she *was* a real princess because only a real princess would have felt the pea through twenty mattresses and twenty eiderdowns. No one except a real princess could be as tender-skinned as that.

So the prince married her, for now he knew for certain that she was a true princess. As for the pea, it was placed in a museum, and you can still see it there, unless someone has taken it away.

How about that for a real story!

Salt Dough

You will need:
2 cups all-purpose flour
1 cup + 2 tablespoons salt
1 tablespoon vegetable oil
¾ cup + 2 tablespoons water

Large bowl, round-ended knife, rolling pin, cookie cutters, baking tray, wire rack, paints, paintbrush

1. Mix all the ingredients together in the large bowl using a knife. The dough should be elastic—add a little more water if needed.
2. Turn the dough onto a floured surface and knead it until it is very smooth and springy.
3. Roll it out with the rolling pin.
4. Cut it into shapes or break pieces off and mold it.
5. Ask an adult to turn the oven on to 350°F.
6. Place the shapes on a lightly oiled baking tray and bake in the center of the oven for about 15 minutes. Smaller items may need a little less time. Bake large items for a little longer.
7. When the shapes are hard, remove them from the oven (ask an adult to help you) and put them on a wire rack to cool.
8. When they are cold, your shapes are ready to paint.

Note: Microwave ovens are not suitable for baking salt dough.

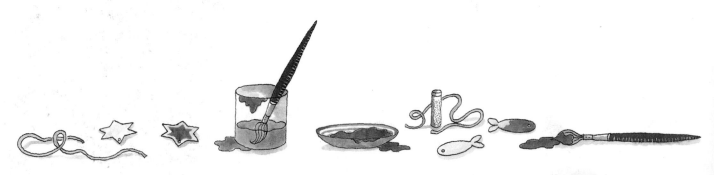

Salt Dough Earrings

Using the salt dough recipe on page 34 make yourself some earrings fit for a princess.

You will need:
Salt dough, cutters, pencil, baking tray, paints, paintbrush, ribbon or string

1. Make some salt dough (follow steps 1, 2 and 3 on page 34).
2. Cut out some shapes—two of each sort. Try some stars, triangles, circles and diamonds. Make some animals, too, such as birds or fish.
3. Using the pointed end of a pencil, make a hole about ¼ inch across in the top of each shape.

4. Bake your earrings as described on page 34 (steps 5, 6 and 7).
5. When they are cool, paint and decorate them.
6. Cut small pieces of ribbon or string. Thread them through the holes and knot the ends to make loops.
7. Hang them on your ears!

Salt dough can be stored uncooked for as long as you like. Just place it in a plastic bag in the fridge. If the dough seems too soft when you take it out, knead some flour into it.

Salt Dough Decorations

Follow the instructions for making earrings on page 35, but make Holiday shapes—bells, stockings, fir trees, angels or stars. Make some loops for them out of ribbon and you can hang them on the Christmas tree or on a coat hanger.

Painting and Decorating Salt Dough

You can use powder, poster or watercolor paints or felt-tip pens on your salt dough shapes.

You could also decorate your salt dough shapes by gluing dried pasta, beads or glitter on to them.

Little Raindrops

Aunt Effie – Jane Euphemia Browne

I am very good Sometimes

Oh, where do you come from,
 You little drops of rain,
Pitter patter, pitter patter,
 Down the window pane?

They won't let me walk,
 And they won't let me play,
And they won't let me go
 Out of doors at all today.

They put away my playthings
 Because I broke them all,
And then they locked up all my bricks,
 And took away my ball.

Tell me, little raindrops,
 Is that the way you play,
Pitter patter, pitter patter,
 All the rainy day?

They say I'm very naughty,
 But I've nothing else to do
But sit here at the window;
 I should like to play with you.

The little raindrops cannot speak,
 But "pitter pitter pat"
Means, "We can play on *this* side,
 Why can't you play on *that?*"

Jonah and the Whale

Retold from The Old Testament,
Book of Jonah

One day Jonah had a quarrel with God.

"Go to Nineveh, Jonah," said God, "and tell the people to mend their wicked ways." Nineveh was a huge city and its people were very wicked indeed. Jonah didn't want to go. So he decided to run away, and got on a ship heading in the other direction.

But as soon as the ship set out to sea, a terrible storm blew up. The sailors were terrified and Jonah felt very guilty. He knew the storm was his fault. He decided to tell the sailors about his quarrel with God.

"Throw me overboard," he said, "then God will stop the storm."

The sailors tried to row ashore instead, but the storm kept forcing them back and in the end they had to give up.

"Sorry, Jonah," they said, and they picked him up and threw him into the sea. Straight away the storm cleared. The sailors were very impressed with Jonah's God.

Of course, God didn't really want Jonah to die; he only wanted to give him a fright. So he sent along a huge whale which swallowed Jonah up in one gulp.

Jonah spent three whole days and nights sitting inside the whale. It wasn't much fun, and he prayed to God, saying he was sorry and promising to do as he was told from now on.

Then God had mercy on Jonah. He told the whale to swim ashore and open its great mouth and Jonah walked out blinking into the sunlight.

"*Now* will you go to Nineveh?" said God.

"Yes," said Jonah, "I will," and he walked all round Nineveh, shouting, "Repent your sins or your city will be destroyed!"

The people believed him, and everybody repented, even the king. God saw that they were truly sorry, and he forgave them. That made Jonah very cross. "How can You forgive them?" he asked. "They ought to be punished!" and he went and sat outside the city and sulked.

As Jonah sat there, God made a tree grow up to shade him from the sun. Jonah liked that. But the next day God made the tree wither away, and Jonah felt sorry for it.

Then God said to Jonah, "You feel sorry for one little tree. Shouldn't I feel sorry for all the thousands of people in Nineveh?"

And Jonah didn't have an answer to that.

Jonah's Breakfast Eggs

1. Fill the saucepan with water and add a pinch of salt.
2. Ask an adult to turn on the stove and put your water on to boil.
3. Meanwhile, take an egg and hold it carefully, pointed end up.
4. With your pen or crayon, draw Jonah's face and hair on the eggshell. Repeat with the other eggs or do other characters.

5. Put your egg on a tablespoon and gently lower it into the boiling water—ask an adult to help you.
6. With your watch, time 10 minutes, then ask an adult to remove your egg with the spoon. This will make a hard-boiled Eggy Jonah. For a soft-boiled Jonah, boil for only 4 minutes.
7. Pop Jonah in an egg cup and slice off the top of his head. Toast strips or buttered bread taste good with your Eggy Jonah.

Jonah Grows Hair!

When you have eaten your Eggy Jonah, why not wash the shell out and make Jonah grow some hair?

mustard and cress seeds

"This is what you'll need..."

cotton

egg box

scissors

clean, empty eggshell

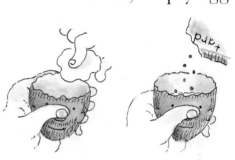

1. Cut one section from the egg box.
2. Place a dampened piece of cotton into the bottom of the empty eggshell and place the eggshell into the egg box section.
3. Sprinkle the mustard and cress seeds on to the cotton.
4. Place on a window sill and remember to keep the cotton damp.
5. In a couple of days the mustard and cress seeds will begin to sprout. Soon Jonah will have green hair!
6. Cut his hair and eat it with some egg sandwiches.

"Goldie thinks she's a whale!"

"He looks good enough to eat!"

"Time for a hair-cut, Jonah!"

The Story of Flying Robert

Dr Heinrich Hoffmann

When the rain comes tumbling down
In the country or the town,
All good little girls and boys
Stay at home and mind their toys.
Robert thought,"No, when it pours,
It is better out of doors."
Rain it *did*, and in a minute
Bob was in it.
Here you see him, silly fellow,
Underneath his red umbrella.

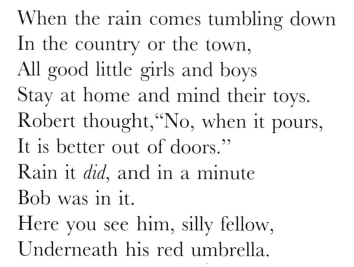

What a wind! Oh! how it whistles
Through the trees and flowers and thistles!
It has caught his red umbrella;
Now look at him, silly fellow,
Up he flies
To the skies.
No one heard his screams and cries,
Through the clouds the rude wind bore him,
And his hat flew on before him.
Soon they got to such a height,
They were nearly out of sight!
And the hat went up so high
That it really touched the sky.
No one ever yet could tell
Where they stopped or where they fell:
Only, this one thing is plain,
Bob was never seen again!

When Fishes Set Umbrellas Up

Christina Rossetti

When fishes set umbrellas up
   If the rain-drops run,
Lizards will want their parasols
   To shade them from the sun.

The peacock has a score of eyes,
   With which he cannot see;
The cod-fish has a silent sound,
   However that may be.

No dandelions tell the time,
   Although they turn to clocks,
Cat's cradle does not hold the cat,
   Nor foxglove fit the fox.

Elena and the Black Geese

There lived once in Russia a young girl called Elena.

One day Elena's mother said to her: "Your father and I are going to the market today, so you must be sure to stay in the house while we are gone, and look after your baby brother. Keep a close watch on him, for the black geese have been seen flying over the village, looking for children to steal. When we return we will bring you some cakes as a reward."

Elena's mother and father set off, and Elena stayed inside with her little brother. After a while she became bored with this and went outside to play with her friends. Remembering her mother's words, however, she took her brother with her and sat him down on the grass so that she could watch over him as she played.

Soon she was completely taken up with her friends' games. When they ran off to play elsewhere, she ran with them, and forgot all about her brother. A moment later the black geese flew over. They swooped down and carried the baby away.

When Elena came back to the house, she looked everywhere for her little brother, and called his name, but there was no sign of him. She became very anxious, and asked herself what could have happened to him.

OLEK..!

She decided the black geese must have taken him off to Baba Yaga, the terrible witch of the forest who ate little children, and she knew that she must go after him straight away if she were to save him.

She set off toward the forest, running as fast as she could. As she ran she heard a voice calling, "Elena, Elena, rescue me!" It was a fish, stranded on the bank of a pond and gasping for breath. Elena didn't want to stop running, but she felt sorry for the fish, so she ran back and gently picked it up and placed it in the pond.

"Thank you," said the fish. "You have saved my life and I will do something for you in return." It dived down under the water and surfaced a second later with a shell. "Take this," it said to Elena. "If ever you are in trouble, throw it over your shoulder." Elena didn't see how a shell could help her, but she didn't want to hurt the fish's feelings, so she took the gift and put it safely in her pocket. Then she ran on.

As she reached the forest and entered the dark canopy of the trees, she saw a squirrel caught in a trap. The squirrel called to her: "Elena, Elena, help me. I will die if you do not set me free."

Elena did not want to stop again, but she could not leave the squirrel to die. She bent down and released it. The squirrel thanked her warmly. "Take this acorn," it said. "If ever you are in trouble, throw it over your shoulder."

"Thank you," said Elena, and put the acorn in her pocket.

She ran deeper into the forest and came to a stony ridge where she saw a mouse trying with all its might to shift a stone three times its size.

"Help me, Elena!" called the mouse. "This stone is blocking the way into my hole." Once more Elena felt she had to stop and help. She removed the stone and prepared to run on. But the mouse called her back. "Take this," it said, handing her a pebble. "If ever you are in trouble, throw it over your shoulder." Elena thanked the mouse and put the pebble in her pocket.

Now she was in the heart of the forest. It was sunless and bleak and she wanted to turn and run home. She was not even sure if she would find her brother alive. More stealthily now, she moved forward until she came to a small clearing surrounded by a fence of bones. Within the fence was Baba Yaga's hut, standing on a chicken leg and turning slowly round and round. The black geese were perched on the roof, asleep. Inside, Baba Yaga was also asleep and the sound of her snoring shook the forest. On the floor beside her Elena's little brother was sitting playing with some old bones.

Elena tip-toed into the hut, picked up her little brother and started to run away.

47

But as she left she stepped on a dry twig. It cracked sharply under her foot and woke the black geese, who squawked and clattered their wings until they had woken Baba Yaga as well.

The witch howled with rage. "Bring back my dinner!" she screamed, tearing after Elena on her long, bony legs.

Elena stumbled on, but her little brother was heavy, and the witch gained on her. In desperation, Elena took the fish's shell from her pocket and threw it over her shoulder.

Immediately, a great lake appeared between her and the witch. It was too wide for Baba Yaga to go round, so she knelt by the bank and drank the whole lake dry in one long, noisy gulp.

In no time at all, she had caught up with Elena again.

When Baba Yaga was nearly upon her, Elena took the acorn from her pocket and threw it over her shoulder. At once a huge forest sprang up, separating her from the witch.

Baba Yaga cursed loudly. The forest was too dense to go through, so she tore up the trees with her bare hands and snapped the trunks with her teeth. Soon not a single tree was left standing.

When Elena looked back and saw the forest all gone, and the terrible witch bearing down on her, she was sure now that she would be caught. There was only the pebble left to protect her. She took it out of her pocket and threw it over her shoulder. To her astonishment, an enormous range of mountains appeared behind her, so tall they touched the sky. They were too high for Baba Yaga to go over, too wide to go round, and she couldn't eat her way through them. She screamed and cursed for some hours, before returning empty-handed to her hut.

Meanwhile Elena walked safely home with her little brother, and was playing happily with him when her parents returned from the market with the cakes.

Baba Yaga's Slippery Snakes

This makes 25 snakes...

You will need:
½ cup + 2 tablespoons
   all-purpose flour
pinch of salt
½ teaspoon mustard powder
½ stick soft margarine, cut into little pieces
½ cup grated cheddar cheese
1 egg, beaten
sesame seeds for decoration

Sifter, bowl, knife, tablespoon, fork, baking tray, pastry brush, wire rack

1. Ask an adult to turn the oven on to 400°F.
2. Sift the flour, salt and mustard together.
3. Rub the margarine into the flour mixture with your fingertips, until the mixture looks like fine breadcrumbs. Stir in the cheese.
4. Add a tablespoon of egg. Use a fork to mix it into a soft dough. You might have to add a little more egg if the dough is not soft enough. Then knead it a little on a floured surface until smooth.
5. Break off small pieces of dough, roll them into sausage shapes and place a little apart on a greased baking tray.
6. Bend them into snake shapes, brush with some of the remaining beaten egg and sprinkle a few sesame seeds on top.
7. Bake for 8-10 minutes until golden brown.
8. Ask an adult to help you remove the tray from the oven and gently lift your finished snakes onto a wire rack to cool.

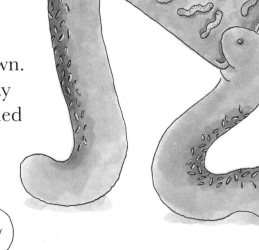

De-li-sss-cious!

Black Geese Finger Painting

You will need a saucer, some finger paint, paper and felt pens to illustrate the story of Baba Yaga and the black geese.

To make Baba Yaga's footprints, pour a little paint into the saucer. Dip the end of your middle finger in the paint and press it down onto the paper to make the front of the foot. Next, dip the end of your little finger in the paint and press it down on the paper to make the heel of the foot. Add little toes with a small paintbrush.

You can also use your fingers to paint a squirrel, a mouse, a fish and the black geese — use felt pens to add the details.

Invisible Writing

white candle or
white wax crayon

paintbrush

This is what you'll need to make some magic!

white paper

paint (for the person receiving the letter)

1. On your piece of paper, write your message with the wax crayon or candle.
2. Send your message to your friend.
3. Your friend must take some paint and, using one color, paint thinly over the paper.
4. The message will appear like magic!

Izzy-wizzy. Get your paintbrush busy!

Magic Painting

paintbrush

thick black paint

wax crayons

paper

You'll need this...

1. Take your wax crayons and
   color a sheet of paper with
   different-colored stripes.
   Press hard so that the paper doesn't
   show through.
2. Next, brush thick black paint all
   over the paper so that you can't see
   the wax crayon.
3. When the paint is dry, scratch
   a picture in it with the end of your
   paintbrush.
4. The colors will appear like magic!

ABRACATDABRA!

Weather

Eve Merriam

Dot a dot dot dot a dot dot
Spotting the windowpane.
Spack a spack speck flick a flack fleck
Freckling the windowpane.

A spatter a scatter a wet cat a clatter
A splatter a rumble outside.
Umbrella umbrella umbrella umbrella
Bumbershoot barrel of rain.

Slosh a galosh slosh a galosh
Slither and slather a glide
A puddle a jump a puddle a jump
A puddle a pump aluddle a dump a
Puddmuddle jump in and slide!

Whether the Weather Is Wet

Whether the weather is wet,
Or whether the weather is hot,
We'll weather the weather
Whatever the weather,
Whether we like it or not!

SPLAT!

The Eentsy Weentsy Spider

The eentsy weentsy spider
Climbed up the waterspout.
Down came the rain
And washed the spider out.
Out came the sun and dried up all the rain,
And the eentsy weentsy spider
Climbed up the spout again.

PLIP! PLOP!

POTTING
COMPOST

56

Instant Eentsy Weentsy

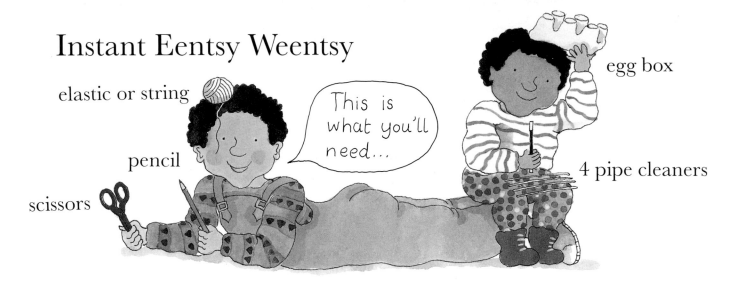

elastic or string

pencil

scissors

egg box

4 pipe cleaners

This is what you'll need...

1. Cut one section from the egg box.
2. With the pointed end of a pencil, poke four holes on each side of the egg-box section.
3. Poke a hole into the top.
4. Take your first pipe cleaner and push it through one set of the holes in the sides. Push the other three pipe cleaners through the remaining holes.
5. Draw a face on your spider with the felt pen.
6. Cut a length of string or elastic and tie a knot in one end.
7. Poke the string through the hole in the top so that the knot is inside.

Hang up your spider... and wait for the screams!

Eek!

57

Alack, Alack, the Clouds Are So Black

Alack, alack, the clouds are so black,
And my coat is so flimsy and thin,
If we further ride on, the rain will come down,
And wet little Sam to the skin.

Brer Anansi and the Rainbow's End

"What a night!" cried Brer Anansi, stomping out of bed. "Rain and thunder all night long! Not a wink of sleep!" He stamped to the window, flung back the curtains—and forgot all about being cross. The rain had stopped, and a rainbow had stretched across the sky: the most perfect, the most dazzling, the most astonishing rainbow he had ever seen.

Then Brer Anansi remembered that rainbows were supposed to have pots of gold at the end of them, and he became so excited that he decided to set off straight away and have a look. He had scarcely gone half a mile when Brer Buzzard swooped down.

"Where are you off to so early in the morning?" asked Brer Buzzard.

"I'm going to the end of the rainbow," replied Brer Anansi, remembering just in time not to mention the pot of gold. He didn't want Brer Buzzard to get there before him. "A good long walk is just the thing on a day like this. Will you join me?"

"Not me!" said Brer Buzzard. "The end of the rainbow is far, far away. I could fly for a year and never get there."

"Good," thought Brer Anansi. "I'll have the gold to myself!"

He wasn't alone for long, though, for Brer Buzzard met Brer Bear as he was flying home, and told him about Brer Anansi's journey. Brer Bear guessed what Brer Anansi was up to, but he just said, "Oh, really? Perhaps I'll follow him."

Brer Buzzard was puzzled. So puzzled, in fact, that he went to talk to Brer Rabbit, even though he and Brer Rabbit always quarrelled, and Brer Rabbit always tried to pull his feathers out.

Now he said to Brer Rabbit: "Brer Anansi and Brer Bear are walking to the end of the rainbow. Why should they do that?"

"How should I know?" snapped Brer Rabbit, reaching out to grab a handful of feathers. "Be gone, you bothersome bird!"

Brer Buzzard flew off. But now Brer Rabbit was puzzled, too. "What are they doing?" he thought. "Perhaps I'll follow them."

By this time Brer Anansi was ready for a rest. He climbed a tree and was dozing in its shade when suddenly he heard a noise. Brer Bear was standing just below him! Brer Anansi sat very still. "I don't want him to find out about the gold," he thought, not realizing that Brer Bear already knew all about it. Then Brer Rabbit appeared, and Brer Bear ran to meet him.

"Are you looking for the rainbow's end?" he asked eagerly.

"No," replied Brer Rabbit. "I just saw you creeping in here and thought I'd see what you were doing. What *are* you doing?"

"I was following Brer Anansi," said Brer Bear, "but I seem to have lost him. Why don't we both look for him together."

Brer Anansi watched as the two set off into the undergrowth, and he decided to eat his lunch. He had just finished when Brer Rabbit and Brer Bear returned, tattered and torn by the sharp thorns and branches. Brer Bear had a sore nose where a bee had stung him. Both were very angry indeed.

"If ever I lay my hands on that Brer Anansi," roared Brer Bear, "I'll teach him not to lead me on such a wild goose chase."

"Me, too," said Brer Rabbit, who had been nipped and nibbled by insects and was more hot and cross than he could ever remember being. "Why don't we go and take a dip in a pond to cool off," he said. "I'm sure we'd feel better."

Brer Anansi waited until they had plunged into the pond, and tip-toed down the tree. Then he crept up to where their clothes were lying on the bank and rubbed itch-bush leaves all over them. "That'll teach them to mind their own business," he thought.

He decided to play another trick on them, too. He ran back to his house, and filled a large pot with pebbles, so that the others would think it was the pot of gold. He ran back to the pond with it, and found Brer Bear and Brer Rabbit in an even worse mood. There were sharp stones at the bottom of the pond, and they had hurt their feet.

"Just let me get hold of that Brer Anansi!" howled Brer Rabbit.

"Why?" asked Brer Anansi innocently. "What have I done?"

"There he is!" shrieked Brer Bear. "After him! Never mind the gold now, let's just skin him alive!" And the two of them leapt out and gave chase, pulling their clothes on as they ran.

Brer Anansi couldn't run very fast because of the heavy pot of pebbles, but he knew he needn't worry. Sure enough, a moment later, Brer Rabbit stopped short. He was itching all over and just couldn't stop! Then Brer Bear started feeling itchy too and he had to stop and scratch and scratch and scratch.

As for Brer Anansi, he ambled home with his pot of pebbles and he laughed and laughed. He hadn't found any gold, but he *had* had fun. And there would be another rainbow another day.

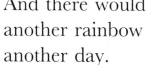

Rainbow Truffles

Spiders eat flies,
Bears eat honey...
But here are some sweets
That are really yummy!

You will need:
2oz. unsweetened chocolate,
  broken into small pieces
2 tablespoons light cream
1 cup confectioners' sugar, sifted
½ cup flaked coconut
multi-colored sugar crystals

Saucepan, heat-proof bowl, wooden spoon, fork, teaspoon,
paper petit four cups

1. Ask an adult to turn on the stove for you.
2. Put about an inch of water in a saucepan.
   Bring it to a boil, then turn off the heat.
3. Place the chocolate in a bowl and rest the bowl
   inside the saucepan against the rim of the pan
   (not touching the water). Stir gently with a wooden
   spoon until the chocolate has melted and is smooth.

4. Remove the bowl from the saucepan and beat the cream and
   confectioners' sugar into the chocolate with a fork. Add the
   coconut and mix well.
5. Cover the bowl and place in the fridge for 10-15 minutes
   until the mixture is firm enough to handle.
6. Gently roll a teaspoonful of mixture in your hands to form a
   ball. Roll it in the sugar crystals to coat it, and place in a
   petit four cup. Repeat until all the mixture is used up.

Brer Anansi's Board Game (for 2-3 players)

You'll need dice and a counter for each player. To make your counters, place a piece of paper over the pictures of the characters on page 65. Trace round the pictures with a pencil and color them in. With some scissors, carefully cut round your traced-out squares to make the counters.

See who gets to the pot of gold first!

24

23
Take a dip
in the pond
Miss a go

22

Jump
over a ditch

21
Go forward
one square

20

19

18

Climb a
creeper

17
Go forward
three squares

Get a lift
from Buzzard

9
Go forward
three squares

10

11

16

Stung by
a bee

15
Go back three
squares

12

14

Tangled in thorns

13
Go back
one square

Brer Anansi

Brer Bear

Brer Rabbit

Doctor Foster Went to Gloucester

Doctor Foster went to Gloucester
In a shower of rain;
He stepped in a puddle,
Right up to his middle,
And never went there again.

The Frog Prince

One fine evening a young princess went into a wood, and sat down by the side of a cool spring of water. She had a golden ball in her hand, which was her favorite plaything, and she amused herself with tossing it into the air and catching it again as it fell. After a time she threw it up so high that when she stretched out her hand to catch it, the ball bounded away and rolled along upon the ground, till at last it fell into the spring.

The princess looked into the spring after her ball; but it was very deep, so deep that she could not see the bottom of it. Then she began to lament her loss, and said, "Alas! if I could only get my ball again, I would give all my fine clothes and jewels, and every thing that I have in the world."

While she was speaking a frog put its head out of the water, and said, "Princess, why do you weep so bitterly?"

"Alas!" she said, "what can you do for me, you nasty frog? My golden ball has fallen into the spring."

The frog said, "I do not want your pearls and jewels and fine clothes; but if you will love me and let me live with you, and eat from your little golden plate, and sleep upon your little bed, I will bring you your ball again."

"What nonsense this silly frog is talking!" thought the princess. "He can never get out of the well; however, he may be able to get my ball for me, and therefore I will promise him what he asks."

So she said to the frog, "Well, if you will bring me my ball, I promise to do all you require."

Then the frog put his head down, and dived deep under the water; and after a little while he came up again with the ball in his mouth, and threw it on the ground. As soon as the young princess saw her ball, she ran to pick it up, and was so overjoyed to have it in her hand again, that she never thought of the frog, but ran home with it as fast as she could.

The frog called after her, "Stay, princess, and take me with you as you promised," but she did not stop to hear a word.

The next day, just as the princess had sat down to dinner, she heard a strange noise, tap-tap, as if somebody was coming up the marble staircase; and soon afterward something knocked gently at the door, and said,

"Open the door, my princess dear,
Open the door to thy true love here!
And mind the words that thou and I said
By the fountain cool in the greenwood shade."

Then the princess ran to the door and opened it, and there she saw the frog, whom she had quite forgotten; she was terribly frightened and, shutting the door as fast as she could, came back to her seat. The king, her father, asked her what had frightened her.

"There is a nasty frog," she said, "at the door, who lifted my ball out of the spring this morning. I promised him that he should live with me here, thinking that he could never get out of the spring; but there he is at the door and wants to come in!"

While she was speaking the frog knocked again at the door, and said,

> "Open the door, my princess dear,
> Open the door to thy true love here!
> And mind the words that thou and I said
> By the fountain cool in the greenwood shade."

The king said to the young princess, "As you have made a promise, you must keep it; so go and let him in."

69

She did so, and the frog hopped into the room, and came up close to the table. "Pray lift me upon a chair," said he to the princess, "and let me sit next to you." As soon as she had done this, the frog said, "Put your plate closer to me so that I may eat out of it." This she did, and when he had eaten as much as he could, he said, "Now I am tired; carry me upstairs and put me into your little bed." And the princess took him up in her hand and put him upon the pillow of her own little bed, where he slept all night long. As soon as it was light he jumped up, hopped downstairs, and went out of the house.

"Now," thought the princess, "he is gone, and I shall be troubled with him no more."

But she was mistaken; for when night came again, she heard the same tapping at the door, and when she opened it, the frog came in and slept upon her pillow as before till the morning  broke; and the third night he did the same; but when the princess awoke on the following morning, she was astonished to see, instead of the frog, a handsome prince gazing on her with the most beautiful eyes that ever were seen, and standing at the head of her bed.

He told her that he had been enchanted by a malicious fairy, who had changed him into the form of a frog, in which he was fated to remain till some princess should take him out of the spring and let him sleep upon her bed for three nights.

"You," said the prince, "have broken this cruel charm, and now I have nothing to wish for but that you should go with me into my father's kingdom, where I will marry you, and love you as long as you live."

The young princess, you may be sure, was not long in giving her consent; and as they spoke a splendid carriage drove up with eight beautiful horses decked with plumes of feathers and golden harness, and behind rode the prince's servant, the faithful Henry, who had bewailed the misfortune of his dear master so long and bitterly that his heart had well nigh burst. Then all set out full of joy for the prince's kingdom, where they arrived safely, and lived happily a great many years.

Just make these puppets and act out the story!

The Pitter Patter Puppet Theater
Proudly Presents...
"The Froggy Prince"

Starring: The Froggy Prince, The Grumpy Princess, The Handsome Prince and The Old King.

This is what you'll need for making your puppets.

four paper bags
newspaper
cardboard
scissors
tape
paints or felt pens
three wooden spoons
three elastic bands

The Froggy Prince

1. Stuff a paper bag with torn-up bits of newspaper. Fold the top of the bag over and tape it down.
2. Draw two large back legs and two smaller front legs on the cardboard.
3. Cut them out and tape them on to the body.
4. Cut out a small crown and tape it on to the top of the bag.
5. Paint your froggy prince and draw him a froggy face.

The Grumpy Princess, The Handsome Prince and The Old King

1. Stuff three paper bags with bits of newspaper.
2. Place each paper bag over a wooden spoon and tie the ends tightly with elastic bands.
3. Cut out three cardboard crowns and tape one onto each head.
4. Paint and draw the princess's eyes, nose, mouth and hair on one paper bag puppet.
5. Do the same for the prince and the king on the other paper bags.

Frog in a Bog

A rib-tickling drink on a hot day!

You will need:
1 orange
2 lemons
1 ½ cups water
½ cup light brown sugar
1 green apple
2 grapes or raisins

Knife, bowl, measuring cup, saucepan, spoon, plate, sieve, chopping board, 3 toothpicks, 4 green drinking straws

1. Scrub the orange and lemons. Cut them in half and squeeze out the juice into a large bowl or jug.
2. Ask an adult to turn on the stove for you. Put ½ cup of water in a saucepan. Bring it to a boil, then turn off the heat.
3. Add the sugar, then the boiling water to the juice (ask an adult to help). Stir well until all the sugar has dissolved.
4. Add the lemon and orange halves and 1 cup of cold water. Cover the bowl with a plate and leave it to cool.
5. Ask an adult to help you strain the juice through a sieve.
6. To make the frog, follow the illustrations below:

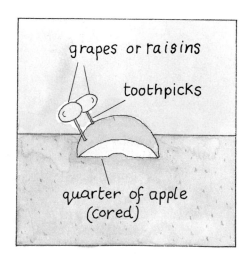

grapes or raisins

toothpicks

quarter of apple (cored)

toothpick   toothpick

glass

juice

Place bendy straws to look like frogs' legs.

ice (optional)

Three Young Rats

Three young rats with black felt hats,
  Three young ducks with white straw flats,
  Three young dogs with curling tails,
  Three young cats with demi-veils,
   Went out to walk with two young pigs
   In satin vests and sorrel wigs;
    But suddenly it chanced to rain,
    And so they all went home again.

75

Happiness

A.A. Milne

John had
Great Big
Waterproof
Boots on;
John had a
Great Big
Waterproof
Hat;
John had a
Great Big
Waterproof
Mackintosh—
And that
(Said John)
  Is
    That.